AUTOBIOGRAPHY
OF AN
ARCHITECT

William House Dove

DEDICATION

I dedicated this book to my wife Jeanette of 62 years without her I could never have made it. Love this, Lady.

In College I was taught that for a book to be readable it must have a great lead in, a strong middle and lastly, an enjoyable ending. I have the first two requirements and only time will judge the ending.

1933 was not a particularly good time to be born, but as fate deals its hand, I was born May 4, 1933, in a duplex residence at 508 Sunset Avenue, Rocky Mount, NC. Delivered by Dr. Hines, to my parents Elmyra House and Billy Hardison Dove. Time of day must have been unimportant. There is extraordinarily little that I know about my early childhood, and little was every discussed with me. I never knew my father as he joined the military and left my life until the late 70's when I discovered my Dove family in South Carolina. My mother was a nurse, and I was raised by my grandparents, "Big Mama" and "Daddy Pop".

POLIO

It was the summer of 1937. Mother and I were going to Myrtle Beach, SC, for a couple of days. It is difficult to remember details, but I do recall that I thought I saw whales in the ocean when in fact it was porpoises swimming offshore (it was sharks). After several days of playing in the Atlantic, we headed back to Rocky Mount so we could head to Florida to visit my Aunt Gertrude and Uncle Clifford. Mother (and my grandmother) did some laundry and then caught the train (Atlantic Coast Line) to Dunnellon, Florida. As with most kids I got bored but welcomed the sight of an elderly lady across the aisle with a bag of candy. With Mothers permission, I had eaten several pieces (I could have eaten the whole bag). Sometime during this (long hour trip), I became nauseated and started throwing up. (Too much candy, Mom thought), and developed a slight fever. Little did we suspect that this was the beginning of infantile paralysis. Finally reaching Florida, ready to leave the train, my leg was asleep, and I could not walk. The Conductor carried me to my waiting Aunt and Uncle. I was hand carried to the home of my kin (Cocowitches), and a doctor was immediately called. After several diagnoses and spinal taps, it was determined that I had a severe disease. This starts my survival of the then unknown – Polio.

A new day. I could not leave Florida for three months and had to have a clearance to enter North Carolina again. Fortunately, I could stay with my kin as my mother (who was a Nurse) had to return to work in the local Hospital. My stay in Florida was uneventful, except I did not have use of the muscles in my left leg. I could move with short crutches, but this was a major learning experience. After returning to NC, it was decided that I should be treated at Duke Hospital, in Durham. Fortunately, I could breathe and only lost the use of my left leg. Doctors decided it would be best to place me in a body cast from my armpits to the ankle of the left side. This was done and maintained for about a year and then I was fitted with a brace. This let me walk with a great deal of difficulty, but I could walk and go as I pleased. This was the second time I learned to walk, and this practice lasted until I was in the second grade (age seven). I was being treated at the Medical College of Virginia, Richmond, VA. (This is where my mother trained to become a registered nurse). After many hours of diagnosis, it was decided that my left ankle needed to be stabilized for a "drop foot". This procedure took place in 1937 at the Hospital in Richmond. Recovery was slow, but effective, and after about a month in the hospital, I could go home. One problem, I had to learn to walk again. (Third time). This time it was a charm. I walked and grew, and walked and grew, and grew. The only challenge in my lifestyle was to be accepted by my peers, as I found out kids can be cruel. I learned to do for myself. If I had a setback, it was back to crutches (no wheelchair) and then try again. During my junior high days, I did not have any major physical problems, only my peers. I developed muscle, and strength and finally wore a leather leg for stability. Finally, with a built-up shoe, I could walk, run, hop, and skip. (New life). Some of my friends did not make it. Polio struck rich, poor, all colors, it did not matter although it was mostly male kids. Early youth, 4, 5, 6 years old. My formative years were enriched in me by my grandparents. Without them I do not know how I would have turned out. As stated earlier, Mom was a Nurse who joined the Army Nurse Corps, and my dad was also in the Military. (Later died in the Panama Canal zone in 1941) I was raised by my Grandparents. (As well as my younger brother, Henry).

We lived in a two-story house on Nash Street, where we shared a second-floor room. This house only had one bathroom and it was in constant use. This house was also shared with my aunt and uncle and one room was rented to two female telephone operators who had irregular hours but was mostly a night shift. My Mother lived in the hospital nursing residence which was one block away. How we survived I do not know. The end of World War II was ending, but everything was rationed. Gas, Shoes, Drinks, Butter (Margarine). We still had convoys traveling down 301 that would block traffic for hours. I always got to be friends with the Military Guards at each corner. Bored them to death wanting to hold their rifles, but they liked me because I would bring them a hot meal and cookies prepared by my grandmother. Food was always an easy entry to fellowships.

After the war, my grandmother was a seamstress for a lady's dress shop, and she made surgery towels for the local hospital. My job was to deliver these and collect money. Sometimes it was as much as two dollars. It bought groceries and minimal clothing, most of my shirts, pajamas were made by "Big Mama" as she was affectionately known. She was a large woman who wore a girder with steel staves. When you got a hug, you got a hug. My Grandad was a small, framed man but had stamina you would not believe. In his healthy days he rode his bicycle to North Rocky Mount, where he was foreman on the construction of the new runway for Rocky Mount Airport. This project was completed under the WPA program with a lot of hand labor.

I learned to ride a bike from him, and it ended up being my passion to be the best rider I could be. I got a bike for Christmas, and it sat in the back hall for over a year while I gathered enough nerve to try. With his help I achieved this goal, although I had to fall into bushes to stop as I had no control over the left side. It didn't matter, I learned to ride with no hands, as well as sit on the crossbar while traveling. This was my "car" and I loved it. It was my transportation for high school, and until college. Mother did get a car my senior year of high school, but I had to park it at the hospital so she could get home the next morning. Mom worked as Head Nurse for the night shift 7:00pm to 7:00am and her salary was the magnificent amount of $ 700.00 a month.

It was my senior year of high school that I met my future wife to be, Jeanette. We dated every chance we had, but she was a lot smarter than me, so I had to study during spare time. We both worked for the local theater and spent most of our free hours on the job. She kept me going and helped me find a way to go to college.

I worked part time as a novice draftsman for a local Architecture Firm, Thompson & Sorrell, Architects. It was during this work that I wanted to be an Architect. I found out that the State had a program to fund individuals for vocational rehabilitation. I applied. Had the required test and examined by four physicians. I qualified. Now what? It only paid tuition and I had to qualify for the School of Design at North Carolina State College, Raleigh, NC. My high school grades were not the best, and I was only taking Algebra I, and I needed Algebra II. My math teacher, Miss Bond, said if I would like she would teach me Algebra II during my lunch hour. What a "god send." I met her every day at 12:00, studied until 12:30/12:45, hurried to my regular job at 1:00 until 5:00, went home to my grandmothers, ate supper, and went to work at the theater at 6:00 until 11:00 (or when the movie was over) Sounds impossible. I had a bicycle. Thanks to Miss Bond I passed and was admitted to NCSD in 1951 with the provision that I take College Algebra, Solid Geometry, and trigonometry during my first quarter as a first-year student. (freshman) Thank God that Math was my best course. You could forget English and its related courses.

I was still dating (going steady) when I packed up and headed for "State", little did I have any hint of what the next five years would surprise me with.

My last year of high school was again a strange factor in my life. My Granddad passed away with stomach cancer, and my grandmother "Big Mama" moved in with my Aunt Freddie and Uncle "A.W.", who had built a home at Sunset Park. Henry and I lived in the big house by ourselves, occupying only one room downstairs and the cold bathroom upstairs. Mother finally found an apartment and the three of us finally moved in together as a family. We moved together several times until we bought a house on Walnut Street and lived there until my brother graduated from high school and later joined the United States Navy.

It was this "home" that we had our first TV, Black and white of course, but you could buy a color applique on the screen to fake color. Big deal, but it satisfied our need as well as our financial ability to pay. Design school was very difficult, but I did make it home often by begging a ride or thumbing passing motorist. Mother had a car, but she could not part with it as often as I wished. I did get it sometimes, which made me the "king" on campus. It was during our time on Walnut Street that my brother had a serious accident while stationed in Newfoundland. During Christmas break from NCS College, I was at home when mother got a telegram stating that my brother was involved in a very serious accident. He and several of his ship mates had been to Argentina, Newfoundland, and Labrador, for moose burgers and beer. On the way back they ran off the mountain side road and landed upside down in a frozen lake, submerged thru the ice layer. Fortunately passing "Newts" tried to extract the sailors from the vehicle. They had to pull hard, and his entire shoulder was dislocated. He was frozen and was carried to the Morgue along with his fellow Navy team. A physician saw his eyes blink and they immediately started a reviving process. It worked but the telegram stated, "We regret to inform you........" Enough said.

I tried the Red Cross for help but to no avail. Being the persistent person that I am, I told Mother I was going to call the Naval Hospital in Argentina. This I did, and the medical staff said they could not give me any information. I then said, May I speak to a patient "Henry Thompson," my half-brother, and wish him a Merry Christmas. Guess who they put on the line. A very weary but alive Henry. Mom and I had a much better Christmas.

After several years, Henry did recover from his mishap, released from the Navy, and returned home to rehabilitate. This story is written to show that I do not believe in giving up. Try every resource available to you, and if not available, invent it.

My college life was basically uneventful because it took my full time to get an education. I did pledge Sigma NU but gave it up because I had a major design project due the weekend that I was to be hazed and inducted. My roommate Norman Bartholomew did get in but I had to pick him up from Umstead Park where he had been dumped covered in syrup and corn flakes (It was only 32° plus). Glad I declined although Miss Annie at the fraternity house was a great cook.

I passed second grade while attending only two months and two weeks, thank God there were teachers like Miss Draper, who really care about their students.

The only sad event during my stay in the hospital was on one of my return check-ups, I was told that Dr. Tucker fell out of the seventh story window and was killed. He sat in the window to smoke while he was talking to his patients. This was a great loss to orthopedic surgeons. The most memorable thing I remember was during a "checkout." Mom was presented a bill for my hospital stay and surgery. Dr. Tucker tore the bill in half and wished me and my mom the best that life has to offer. After Dr. Tuckers death, I continued to go to Richmond every six months for a checkup. Our next-door neighbor drove the Trailways bus to Richmond and I would ride with him (behind the driver's seat and he would let me out at the hospital, into the care of awaiting nurses. He would pick me up for the return trip home at 4:00pm, alone at eight years old. I had caring humans who did all they could for a young, crippled man. To this day I hate the word crippled, as it did not exist in my mind back then, and it does not exist in there today.

Not much happened in my growing experiences until 8th grade when I managed to get expelled from school for allegedly skipping school. I thought I was excused to go with the Rocky Mount High School Football team, where I was assistant, assistant, assistant manager. In other words, I taped star players ankles. Anyway, mother had a friend of my aunt Katherine who lived in Hampton, VA. As fate would have it, she married this guy so me and my brother (I forgot to mention that mother married again and had my brother Henry Thompson. Born when I was 5 years old. But that is another story)

We moved to Hampton, and I finished the eighth and ninth grade at Buck Roe High school. This school was one block from the ocean, and it was exceedingly difficult to try to study.

During these years "Polio," gave me a challenging time, and I had to wear a leather leg that had two steel bars and laced up like a pair of work boots. Nevertheless, I would put this on in the morning, got on the bus, go to school. At school I would take off the leather brace, put it on top of the toilet stalls and replace it in time to catch the bus home. Mom never knew this because she thought I was making remarkable progress.

It was in Hampton, VA, I started building model airplanes, and was a member of the Brain Busters model airplane club. Its youngest member as the rest of the club members were Aeronautical Engineers, all with PHD's. I guess I did not know how lucky I was, because I got to build various models at the NACA Headquarters at Langley Field, VA. I did get to watch Sikorsky work on his helicopter and see the trials of the US's first Jet Plane. The early 1950's were the greatest years ever.

So much for Hampton. Mother got tired of her new husband and wanted to get back to Rocky Mount and nursing.

As I mentioned before, my grandparents raised me. Mother had married the second time and brother Henry was born when I was five years old. I do not remember Henry's dad, except that he worked for the railroad, and delivered coal for his dad who owned Thompson Coal Company on South Church Street. (Sometimes he delivered ice to the various in town residences) Henry Thompson (My brother was Henry Allen Thompson Jr.) was a hard-working individual, who liked to drink and play cards with the rich "guys" in town. Eventually this led to major financial problems and later he committed suicide to escape his life's problems. After that financial hardships set in and mother being a nurse, went back to work and we moved in with my grandparents. Life really began at this point. Grandmother taught us right from wrong, sometimes the hard way. One a particular incident I "borrowed an eighty-nine cent Indian headdress from the local 5 cent 10 cent store. My Grandad walked back to the store with me to return said item. It was only three blocks, but I know it felt like forever before we got there. Daddy Pop paid for misdeed and asked the manager how could I work this dept off? I washed the drinking fountains, both for "colored" and "white" every day, for one month. Debt paid. I was in love with the girls at the candy counter, because they were sympathetic to my transgression. I never stole again.

We moved from 326 Nash Street to 214 Nash Street. An upgrade to a larger house. We had our own room. One bath upstairs, for all. At times, my aunt and uncle lived upstairs. Sometimes, my mom had a room, but she later moved back to the nursing home behind the Rocky Mount Sanitarium Hospital.

It was during the war years that I appreciated America the most. We had many convoys that went down our main street, Church Street, with a soldier stationed at every corner. Sometimes it would take an hour for all the vehicles to pass. The soldiers had guns and full Military uniforms. I was impressed and spent many hours standing and talking with these guys, aggravating them most of the time. Could I hold their rifle, try on the heavy helmets. Of course, it did not bother them when my grandmother would send me to the corner with a "hot" meal which was consumed instantly. Times were tight during those times. Everything was rationed like gasoline as well as butter, rice, clothes, and several other things. My grandad would cut out cardboard insoles for my right shoe when my sole wore out. Finally, rubber for soles came in and I was waterproofed again. We collected metal, tinfoil, and bought war bonds. It was during these years that I practiced my first Architecture. I built a little store in the front yard, out crates and cardboard, from the downtown stores. It was great, had a door, a drop-down counter, was painted solid black, and had one light bulb for light. The store was called

"Little Nothing" and sold candy bars, bubblegum, to phone operators who boarded across the street. I did make a profit, but the city did not like my operation. Somehow, we got thru, and I could stop mixing the capsule in the white margarine to make it yellow.

I continued thru grade school, moved to Virginia for a new stepdad, stepsister, and stepbrother. This only lasted for 9th and 10th grade and I moved back to Rocky Mount to live again with my Grand Parents. Mother got out of the army nursing Corp as a second lieutenant and came back to Rocky Mount to continue her nursing career. During 12-hour night duty and sleeping in the daytime. This gave my brother and me plenty of free time. But we managed to stay out of serious trouble. No drugs or pregnant girlfriends My aunt and uncle built a new home near the Sunset Park, and this left Henry and me in a very large house, occupying one room with kerosene space heater and a very cold upstairs bath. We could have hot water if we put a quarter in the gas meter. What a life. Mother arranged for us to eat at Parkers Restaurant on Nash Street, where we charged our meals and sometimes ate with her for the evening meals.

Not having a chance to go to higher education, Clyde Bailey of Bailey's Jewelry, said he would help me be a watch maker and sought entrance for me in a school in Tennessee. I continued to worry him and Mrs. Bailey as I pursued a high school degree. During this time, I took a course called D.E. Diversified Education, which allowed me to work and go to school. I was taking drafting and one of my teachers found me a part time job with a local Architect, Thompson, and Sorrell, located on the second floor of the downtown Epstein's Building. I rode a bike (my main transportation) to school, to work and back to my grandparents. It was during my senior year of High school that I met Jeanette Stancil. She had assisted in getting me a free train ride back from our Fayetteville football game. It seems my ride down was not coming back to Rocky Mount until Sunday. I had only a few bucks, so I was hidden between two seats in coach class, until the conductor took up tickets. This started a beautiful romance. Both of us worked at the Center theater where I was head usher/door attendant, and she was candy girl and sometimes ticket sales. I made forty-four cent per hour, and she made forty cents. It seems impossible now, but I went to school from 8:00/12:00, ate a candy bar for lunch, rode my bike to Thompson Sorrell, worked from 1:00 to 5:00, rushed to big mamas to have a prepared supper and get to the theater to work from 6:00 to 11:00. Not as bad as it sounds because after the start of the 9:00 movie I had two hours to study.

It was my mid-year of my senior year of high school when a "genie" appeared and presented an opportunity for me to go to college. This was unreal because my family was only one step from being poor. North Carolina had a program called vocation rehabilitation, and if I could qualify, it would pay for my tuition and fees at a state supported institution. I applied and after many interviews I was granted this wonderful opportunity. Now the hard part. I did not have the requirement for admission to North Carolina State College. My algebra teacher Miss Wiita Bond said she would teach me Algebra II During my Lunch hour before I went to work. My lunch hour was now ½ hour, but I was going to pass this course. Without Ms. Bond I would never have attended NC State in the school of design. God bless this lady who turned my life around. My next problem was completing grade 12 and preparing to take college algebra, solid geometry, and trigonometry all together when I arrived at NC State College in September 1951.

We moved from Nash Street to Hammond Street with mother moving with us. Three real family in the same house. Mother had bought a 48 Desoto and I had wheels. Of course, I had to carry mom to work at

7:00pm. Have a date and park the car at the hospital at 11:00 pm and walk home. This was only about 4 blocks. Sometimes, I would go into the hospital and eat pie and coffee with mother and then head home. After several moves, mother bought a small house on Walnut Street. Two bedrooms, one that my brother and I shared and one for mom, who slept during the day. While all this growing experience, I was continuing to see Jeanette and I knew she was the one for me. I pursued this person with a strong passion. She was working during my senior year in High school, but we still had free passes to four theaters, dating was cheap.

I finally graduated from RMSH and was ready for the next big step in my life. Before I left for College, I built a carport on mother's house. My second Architectural project. This one was ugly. But it worked. Our car was dry. Mother bought a new car and Jeanette bought the Desoto. I knew I was seeing a very wealthy young lady.

College was exceedingly difficult for me as buildings were far apart with only 10 minutes between each class. It was nice because I was one of the guys and I fitted in. There were only a few girls on campus in 1951, but I was no longer known as "hop-a-long" or "crip" only plain Bill. Jeanette visited me on Sundays, and some weekends. I came home to clean clothes, money, not linens, they could last an entire quarter. The school of design did not allow much free time, but I did manage to watch a gang at the bowling center and sometimes basketball. This was a hot time for b-ball, with Everette Case as coach in my first, second and third year moved along nicely with no major upsets. The fourth year was where they weened out the weaker students. I know I was not top notch, but my scholarship was for five consecutive years. The battle to stay was not easy but I begged, pleaded, prayed and I continued to the fourth year. Several of my best buddies did not make it. Jeanette and I got married. Our marriage was very unusual in that neither of our parents could provide funds for a large wedding. Jeanette and I were counseled for marriage by a young Baptist associate minister in Rocky Mount. He accepted a pastor position at the Baptist Church in Aulander, NC. So, we went to his church to be married. Two young but energetic souls ready to make a new day and build a new world. We were married August 21, 1954, by Rev. Phillips, his pregnant wife played the organ and two witnesses we had never met before or have met again. The wedding was great. Jeanette in her white dress and me in a seersucker suit. Awaiting a honeymoon at the Pecan Grove Motel, in New Bern, and a destination of Carolina Beach. We were Married!!

Our first big encounter was stopping for a coke and discovering that my new bride had left all her hanging clothes at her house. I said I guess you will have to wear your wedding dress for a week. Not true, we stopped in Williamston, and she bought a white blouse and blue skirt, which had to be altered. My vision of sugar plums was diminished as I waited in the car for an hour. Finally, on our way for a great Honeymoon.

Jeanette moved to Raleigh and found a job at First Federal Savings and Loan. This was the stabilizer in my life. I was spending 18 hours a day in school. Pulling all-nighters and in general wearing out. She had an apartment, brilliant idea. Put the chain on the door at 2:00am and if I arrived later than this. Sleep outside, in the car or with my previous roommates in the basement next door. I did not miss this curfew but ones. It was nice to snuggle up to a warm body that wanted me to succeed. It worked, I finished the fourth year and proceeded to the fifth year. (Graduation from the school of design was a 5-year curriculum). The fifth year was more of the same except more intense and critical. I was fortunate to have visiting lectures from all over the world. Frank Lloyd Wright was my first Contact "Public Lecture" but with great intensity. As the years moved on, we had lectures by Pier Nervi, William

Duduk, Robert Le Ricolais, Roberto B Mark, and my favorite Richard Neutra. Also, we were taught by Buckminster Fuller while building a Geodesic dome using cardboard structural members. This unit had to have the capability of being lifted by helicopter and flown to the state fairgrounds. I had the privilege of flying in the chopper, praying that cable didn't break or that unit did not totally disintegrate. We made it and the unit was a success, and the army had their new field headquarter structure.

Graduation finally occurred late May and I graduated with a Bachelor of Architecture Degree. Sixty kids started in 1951, with only 5 of the original class graduating in five years, 1956. We had 24 students in my class, but most of those were transfers in and out over the years. I was now prepared to design the largest, tallest, costliest buildings in the United States.

Shortly after graduating, I qualified to sit for the Architectural registration exam. During the summer, I had completed part of the three-year experience requirement.

Starting on Monday, June 11th, I packed up my pencils, "T" square, triangles, and 5 years of knowledge, I was ready. Two exams Monday, one eight hours on Tuesday, one exam on Wednesday, and finally a 12-hour exam on design. You could not have books, only a slide rule, and all activities were monitored, even toilet breaks. Thanks to the local church ladies, who sold sandwiches, drinks, and sugar items, you could get through 12 hours. Exams over, Jeanette picket me up, and we headed to the beach. I was on the rear seat, partially dead, but thankfully it was over. Beach and rest were great, but we needed to move back to Rocky Mount, where I was to be employed by Thompson Sorrell, Architects, who had promised me a junior partnership when I had my Architectural license. After relocating back to riverside apartments and Jeanette going to work for Planters Bank, I was notified that I had passed all the exams in one sitting. I only needed 3 months of office practice and I was the youngest Architect in North Carolina. What a day to be assigned license number 1029. This number was to appear on over 800 projects and hopefully a few more as I reach 77 years old.

The real story begins here, January 1ˢᵗ, 1957.

We settled in at 506 Darden Court, a nice two bed unit. Floor Furnace, no Air Conditioning, but the best young neighbors you could ask for. We were all recently married and beginning a career. Jeanette made the light deposit, and one month's rent, $55, and I started to work for Thompson & Sorrell, Architects. Small office, the three of us, but a lot of enthusiasm. My salary to start was $85, a week. No fringes, but I had a job. Things went well for a while, but I sensed I was not going to become a partner. Things had moved to fast for John and Russ, to give up a piece of the action. During this time, I reacquainted a relationship with Ryland Edwards. He was taking the Architectural Exam during the same time that I sat for it. Jeanette was pregnant and I needed to seek a better future. Our first child was born in August 1957, Jeanette could not work at the bank after she was three months pregnant (showing). Decision time for me to look at a better paying position. Ryland and I struck up a stronger friendship, and I committed to work for Harless and Edwards for $110 per week. I departed Thompson and Sorrell after hiring Dan Knight to take my place. Dan had worked during the summer and was still in school but would graduate several years later from NCSU in Architecture.

Little did I know that Harless and Edwards were in financial trouble. I owned 22% of the firm by default, through a salary adjustment plan. My first chore, find out the problem, instigate and analyze and provide a solution. The elder female receptionist/bookkeeper had not balanced the bank account or posted to the ledger for over two years. With Jeanettes help I took the bank account and ledger home, and we started work at our dining table at 6:00 pm and by 2am we had things balanced. I learned office accounting procedures in a one night sitting.

My next chore was to convince Harry Harless, (the senior partner) to let our front office staff go. She had been with the firm for over ten years. My first job as office manager was to terminate her employment with the firm. This was not pretty, my first firing. After clearing this hurdle, I reduced all our salaries, totaled up our liability, and our few assets. It took two years and several nice projects to get Harless and Edwards on solid financial grounds. During this time, we hired Dan Knight who was having financial problems at Thompson and Sorrell. During the first years with my association and ownership in Harless and Edwards, I was fortunate to become associated with Carolina Telephone Company, in Tarboro. They had an Architect working on a new building in Downtown Wilson, and he could not seem to get the drawings produced. Mr. CR Jones, Vice President of Carolina Telephone had heard of me from a local contractor. D.J. Rose & Son. I met with CR Jones and told him our office could produce these drawings in thirty days. This we did and he provided me with continuing service contract for all buildings, etc. required by Carolina Telephone. This contract started in 1957 and lasted until the Early 2000. Any firm would be thankful for this type of contract. (As a sidebar, this contract led to our association with General Telephone, located in Durham) This contract was for all work in NC, SC,

VA, W.VA, Kentucky, TN, Alabama. Wow, what a career even though I stayed in an airplane a lot of this time.

Harless and Edwards dissolved when Mr. Harless decided to semi-retire. The new firm was Edwards Dove and Knight. This firm lasted until 1977 when it became, Dove, Knight & Associates, PA. Our firm could have been much larger, but at my insistence we stayed with staff of 8-10. Comfortable size for Eastern North Carolina. A large firm approached out of New Jersey to head up their Architectural Department. I could have an increased salary, a residence only one hour away by train, and a country club membership. After one week of consideration, my decision was to stay in Rocky Mount. I could be at work in one ½ minutes and on the golf course in less than 10 minutes with a whiskey sour in my cart.

After making this decision, it was time to have a professional home for the business. My former two partners did not care to be involved in this endeavor, so I bought a lot on Stony Creak from RC Branch (our next-door neighbor) and with the help from Planters Bank. I built a building at 3136 Zebulon Rd. This was a new concept for construction. D.J. Rose, Inc put in foundation poured slabs and erected the steel frame, Precision walls from Raleigh did all the exterior, interior, walls, and finishes. It was really a lot of fun, except, Zebulon Road stopped in front of our office, and remained a dead end for many years. Private offices, for partners, and a large drafting room for staff. We even had a gas fireplace in the conference room. We were on our way. My three children (yes, three) owned the facility under the title of LJW Enterprises (first letters of kid's names). This building actually paid for itself three times in thirty years. The Architectural office had some difficult years for a while but overall, it was successful with a steady client base.

During this maturing time, I was invited to attend a meeting concerning Saxon Oil Company, by owners of Boddie-Noell (Hardees Franchisers) I could invest $10,000 in oil exploration and possible future revenue. This was a successful gamble. Jeanette and I borrowed the money and Saxon did the rest. The well-produced and we put the money in a Clifford trust for 10 years and a day. This income paid for my three kids to attend college. Again, a wise decision. Not all my investments were successful. I had some bad ones, but Uncle Sam took care of these.

Edwards, Dove, Knight and later Dove, Knight had great staffs. As a reward and a learning experience, we took trips to New York, Washington, DC, and over 10 tropical Islands, including Bermuda. These trips were for long weekends. Husband and wives included. Your staff is your life blood. We were fortunate to train over ten future Architects. (We trained our competition) But each one was worth its friendship.

As I grow older, I still have a passion for architecture. I was never as good as I wanted to be, but I do have several buildings, which make me proud, and a lot of loyal friends and associates. Friendship does not have a monetary value, but I think I will have enough to be pall bearers.

At 76 I started again, and have only one staff member, a truly bright young lady from Holland with a potential future that is unlimited.

My life is very full of a wife, two daughters, one son, one granddaughter and two grandsons, reasonably good health, and intriguing practice, what more could a guy expect.

Now for the Fun Stuff!

Fun Stuff, 1954 thru 2000.

Life is short, but you can put a lot of time in fun stuff if you budget yourself. I did not learn this path easily. As stated earlier I married Jeannette on August 21, 1954, and if two people could "build" a life it was us. My practice (young and inexperienced) offered me many opportunities for this young NCSU graduate. Jeanette provided most of the support after we were married. I worked summers and weekends to help with a real financial burden. It was necessary for me to work long hours (sometimes too long). But it was a means to a stable future. Salary of $110 per week did not go far (but remember our first car was a Plymouth Plaza, light blue, but it carried us well and had automatic transmission. When her salary stopped and we were living in a two-bedroom apartment and with me being so productive, we had two girls and a boy on the way. Time to build a home. We were buying a lot in Englewood for $2,500 and had made several payments. Mr. Z.B. Bulluck owned the lots as well as the building we were renting from him on Forest Hills Ave. Only I would think that I could ask him for the title to 309 Englewood drive and still make payments to him. To my great surprise he said yes, and we were on our way. I had a free hand for design, colors, size, everything, because Jeanette was pregnant with Billy, and we had to move. Billy was born on April 15, 1962. Three kids and a new home our little family was complete. Riverside apartments had been good to us, good lasting friends, and neighbors. Home was ready, and now payments started. Little did I know that I would later add to this home several times, and never move or build again.

Kids grew and went to various public schools, until situations presented themselves for me to decide on private education facilities. Dancing, piano, ballet, sports, kept us all busy all the time. Jeanette played tennis and hauled kids everywhere. Had to get a second car. Ordered a Honda Civic No of 2060 price $3,300, gas shortage made this the correct decision. It was yellow and lasted until Billy completed college in 1985.

We did not splurge, but we did work on a budget, so we could enjoy our world. We carried the kids to Expo sixty-seven in Canada. Could not speak French, but soon learned enough to survive. Two weeks in Montreal, but we saw and learned a lot. Next trip was Hemisfair in Texas, and trips to Key West, Hot Springs Ark, Six Flags GA and to be not outdone for history all of us went from Murphy to Manteo for two weeks to see our wonderful state of NC.

While all kids were in High School and Freshman College, we took off for Hawaii for a week in our remote state. This was also with two hundred Alumni headed by Bryce Younts, Alumni Director.

All kids have graduated from college, and still have the urge to travel. As each kid married, we provided a Honeymoon trip to Bermuda. Jeanette and I had been several times and really loved it very much. I even went with my brother one time. Played golf, toured a lot and one trip Jeanette and I visited a mariner's museum where we met a caretaker dressed as a pirate, wooden leg, and all. He was carrying a sack of cement (94lbs) and told me he could make me a wooden leg like his and I would be able to carry this kind of load. I politely told him I would keep my leg as I did not care to carry that much load.

Probably one of my best trips was to Europe in 1997 with my son, Billy. Jeanette did not care to travel on water (in a big boat) so I convinced Billy to go with me. (This was not a too tough arm twisting. We left Raleigh on a trip that was a trip. We had no clue as to what to do or when to do it. Landing in New York was a real "hello." We were met by a limousine to carry us to the dockside of the Queen Mary II. This was a big ship, but we managed to hop on board and greet our captain and other staff. We were escorted to our "state room" to get ready for necessary sailing instructions. Our Stateroom was large, six feet by six feet, with a midget shower toilet and a small port hole, but it was our home for five days. I never knew that I could meet so many people but we both did.

At our table was the vice president of General Motors with his wife and a young couple from Scotland on their second honeymoon. Talk about "high cotton" We were in it. Billy could make friends with the devil, and he did. Playing tricks on the young couple and "sucking up" to the V.P. We also did not have any problem with the wine steward (she was pretty and British.

If you have never sailed on a large ship, it is a fantastic experience, and an experience you will cherish always. The crew and all staff were very well trained to make you feel comfortable. I tried all types of food as long as it contained beef, and I did not know you could have so many drinks and still walk. Of course, if the ship was listing to port, it helped me walk. Just Kidding.

Billy, me, several people, and friends to be at poolside. One individual happened to be Tom Clancy, who had just completed his new book. We had to have a copy and our picture taken, with him. Both of us had rather been photographed with the very attractive young lady traveling with him. This famous author said it would make us "immortal" (I may have spelled this incorrectly). Good writers and a great conversationalist. We did visit him a few more times during our on-deck time.

We also visited and had a book signed by Helen Forrester "Mourning Doves" (thought this would be appropriate for Jeanette)

Possibly the most educational part of our sailing trip was on board. A crew from the British Airways who were pilots, for the Concord. Billy and I were to fly the Concord back to the US from Paris. I attended every lecture and was amazed at what this great airplane could do. I knew it was fast but had no idea what Mach II meant. It was explained beautifully along with a thousand details as to what made it fly twice the speed of sound, and that it grew one foot in length, during this flight. Much later in this story, but now back to the QE2 We both had a ball, especially at the pool deck where the lady from Denmark put on a show every day at 10:00am. She also had a lovely four-year-old daughter. Other than the ship itself, I was completely taken back while sailing past the statue of liberty at dusk, beautiful, and under neath the Verrazzano-Narrows Bridge. The last land we saw for five days. The Atlantic Ocean does get boring, and you wish for the sighting of land. We finally saw seaweed and sea gulls. What a thrill. We also saw large sailing vessels and knew we were close to South Hampton England. We docked at night, so I was incredibly surprised to look out our only daylight port hole and see a large ship docked next to us. We had said our goodbyes at dinner last night, had our clothes cleaned, we were now ready for London. My baggage handler (Billy) retrieved our luggage and away we went. Our accommodations in London (Langham Hilton) were great. Center of everything and across the street from the Royal Academy of British Architects. Did not visit because architecture was way of the radar. We ate British food for the first time. Just O.K., our plans were to visit the known attractions, but as usual for me, I obtained the services of local taxi for the day.

Early our first day we went to the Cathedrals (St. Paul's and Westminster) and spent half the morning looking at the Architecture. I did get to say hello to Sir. Christopher Wren at St. Paul's and stepped on T.S. Elliot's Grave at Westminster.

I am still amazed that the German U-2 did not bring this building down. It only struck in one leg of the support arch but did not explode. God was looking out for this magnificent structure.

I had written a thesis on the great fire of London and had to see the campanile that marked this point in pudding lane. Billy was not too impressed with my choices of visits, but I did treat him to lunch at Harrods Department Store. Two steak sandwiches with tea and a go to toilet coupon. Girls playing piano, but Rolex watches were prize. We functioned as if we were purchasing a nice watch, but I think $20,000 was a bit out our range. A Beer on the sidewalk after playing in the toy section for a while was a pleasure. After dinner we went to "cats" at the Llyod Webber Theater. Again, a magnificent experience. The third day we went to Bath for the Roman Antiquities, and again I saw this exciting Architecture. After Bath we took a trip to the "Stonehenge" could not believe it in person. Big and beyond how they did it. In the US we have trouble lifting concrete beams. Billy walked around and took some nice photographs. He was impressed also.

Back to London for rest and dinner and prepare for our trip to Paris.

Everyone should take the fastest train I had been on, under the English Channel and through the beautiful fields of France. The trip was quick, but Paris awaited us for our final leg. Three days to see everything (impossible).

Again, I secured a cab for us for our daily excursion. Picked us up at 9:00am and we were on our way to Notre Dame. Too crowded for an Architect but a wonderful place for pick pockets to operate. The structure and stain glass were superior to what I had imagined. Still liked the statue of a male carrying his head, but this is another story. Billy and I sat in the gardens to take in the full understanding of flying buttresses. We walked down several blocks along the Seine River, to look at all the artisan's work. What a gallery, we needed several hours. Our cab was waiting so we continued our trip. First gold dome of the invalids. Rodin's gardens where you could see his sculptures including the famous "the thinker." After looking at gardens, we took in the rest of the tourist attractions. On the Champs Elysees with its sidewalk cafes, shops, and Architectural masterpieces. Lunch was simple but great, and this is where Billy bought sexy lingerie for his girlfriend. My destination for the day was the Picasso Museum where I spent a few hours. At one time I owned a Picasso print and a large terra cotta plate with a painting of a "big bird" on it. I later donated this to NCSU.

The last stop was to see I.M. Pei Pyramid at the Louvre and drive by the small replica of the statue of liberty on an Island facing exactly to our own in New York. Our driver kept asking why I want to see this. Because I did. Our day ended back at the hotel which was located less than one block to the Eiffel tower. Really impressive steel structure, and it survived World War II.

I hated that our short visit to Paris was about over, we decided we must see Moulin Rouge Theater. This we did on our last night with dinner and a great show. Billy became sick and returned to the hotel. Not sure if he was sick or liked the French girls on each corner, I stayed and was pleased with the show, meal, and companions at the table.

I Save The Best for Last.

When the Concorde was starting its flights. I was determined that one day I would be on board. That day came in 1997 and it was more than I ever dreamed about. The waiting VIP area was exquisite, beautiful furniture, beautiful French female attendants and food and drinks of your choice. Fresh squeezed orange juice, coffee, French pastries. An attendant walk with you to the awaiting plane. No rush, only plain service that I have not seen duplicated on any of my trips.

We take our seats. (Billy next to the window and me on an aisle.) Seats two seats per aisle maximum of one hundred passengers, plus flight crew. Before takeoff we had wine and pastries. Our flight attendees change from uniforms into dresses, neck scarves, high heels. I knew this was going to be all and more than I expected. As we "took off" we were traveling at runway speed of 260 MPH. Once air born, we reached the ocean where the noise from breaking the sound barrier would not be a problem. When we reached twice the speed of sound a monitor let us know and soon, we would be at 58,000 feet altitude. More wine, dinner, more wine, desert, more wine. Billy was still not feeling well so he was not in the best mood, but I did not care. I was as close to heaven as I might get. I was in my dream world. The flight was quick to New York. Just over three (3) hours. With 98% of our fuel used up, we landed with cockpit nose down, so pilot could see. Billy got our luggage and we traveled from LaGuardia to JFK for our last flight home. This was a small plane, twenty seats, and bumped us all over the sky, finally back in Raleigh I said to the pilot that we had flown in chicken salad to chicken shit.

As far as a fun thing, this had to have been one of the best. Several weeks gone from work, seeing the beautiful sights of our world, eating foods and wines of unknown origins, and finally, spending time with my runner, Mr. security agent, my baggage masters my shipmate, my confident, my son "Billy".

In the "fun" things in a career, I failed to mention one of the best. In 1995, I was elected president of the NCSU Alumni Association. After serving many years on the board, my fellow Alums felt it was time to honor me with this position. The year that followed were terrific as this was the last time frame that the Alumni Association would act as an independent identity. We became an arm of the University with our leader being a vice president of NCSU. Up until this time our director was Bryce Younts. Bryce was the most fantastic person I had ever met. He knew all alums by name, where they were from, and how many kids they had. The loss of this man with his assets, was a "blow" to all our alumni friends. I am sure he is looking down to see what the red and white are doing to strengthen our university.

Not much happened in the early two thousand. Business was still flourishing, but I was beginning to tire from the day-to-day operations. So, I decided that Jeanette and I would take off a month and travel the United States. Our trip began in Rocky Mount, and we traveled south ward to the Memphis area where we could gamble, rest and head on to Texas had to see the buried Cadillacs. Then to New Mexico to see my aunt Katherine (now deceased) in Albuquerque. Our trips are long, but

I broke them into 300/400 miles per day drive. We stayed in Laughlin Nevada, ate in the West most Cracker Barrel, and gambled a lot. Without any luck at the machines. We headed to the coast of California for a drive north to San Francisco. Our plans changed by the forest fires. We did not get into Yosemite because of the terrible traffic "back-ups," so just stuck to ocean drive and after spending several nights, we ended in San Francisco. What a disappointment, we were at the wrong place at the wrong time, but I did drive across the Golden Gate Bridge, and was totally amazed by this structure. What an amazing structural design.

We were going to go west to Jackson City but had to divert north due to forest fire smoke. This ended up being a great adventure. Because we went to Idaho and entered Yellowstone Park thru the west gate. This was great. We could tour south, the lava pits and finally "Old Faith full Geyser." On our next day we could head north, see the forest, waterfalls and eventually end up in Cody, Wyoming. While in Cody, we had to see a live rodeo. The wind blew a hundred miles per hour, and we had a tough time standing up. Really a great show, and beautiful horsemanship.

Leaving Cody, we headed to the north as I had an appointment for a tour of "Fallen Waters" designed by Frank Lloyd Wright. I could not miss this treat as I had been driving for a month to arrive in Pennsylvania on time. We did stop to see the Corn Palace, as well Mount Rushmore, and Crazy Horse Rock Carvings. We did not miss Sturgis, South Dakota, home of the motorcycle event of the year.

Finally arriving at "Falling Waters," we were treated like royalty. Hostess called our name, and we were picked up in a van for the short but difficult travel to the house. What a structure. Pictures are great but seeing it firsthand extremely rewarding. I had seen Taliesin lodge years earlier, but this was breath taking. I was told I could stay as long as I wished and go where I wanted. They were reworking the concrete terraces and I got to see the original design, as well as the restoration. We could have stayed for days, and I would not have seen all of Wrights details. We called for the van and headed back to the visitor center, and I thanked the staff for their hospitality. I had a renewed respect for Architecture, and design, and decided I would work a few more years to see if I could become famous (still waiting).

This fun trip was about over but we stopped in Harpers Ferry and Charlestown, West Virginia to gamble. I had also designed buildings in these two towns for the General Telephone Company of the Southeast.

The last four-hour drive back to Rocky Mount was really boring, but we had seen the United States of America, North, South, East and West. What a country.

My practice started in 1957.

A nd with a few lean years, I would say that it has been successful for a small-town architect. It has allowed me to expand my knowledge, my family, my personal holdings and given me a real sense of purpose. My firm has designed many significant buildings, maybe not famous, but in the eyes of our clients a successful solution to their building requirements.

One last fun time was our trip to Nova Scotia. This trip carried up the East Coast, thru New York, Maine and into Canada. Our visit to Halifax was dramatic after having driven thru vast beautiful landscapes without any buildings. You could drive fast. (No traffic or towns.) While in Halifax, we took side trips to Peggy's Cove (famous lighthouse), and the site of the Swiss Flight plane crash, with no survivors, in St. Margaret s Bay. On this trip, we did not go to Prince Edwards Island, and this was truly a mistake. On our last night, we went to the casino and paid our taxes in Nova Scotia. Leaving Halifax, we headed north to the St. Lawrence River for a drive to Montreal, while passing thru Quebec City. This was really a beautiful drive, and we stopped several times to eat. From Montreal, we headed south towards home. Having always loved baseball, we stopped in Coopers Town, for a visit to the baseball hall of fame facility, and then back to Rocky Mount, NC. Lots and lots of miles but each one was a wonderful experience that can be tucked back in memory for later recall.

All the fore going story sounds at times as a fairy tale. Each year of your life, you have some difficulties. In my life, I have enjoyed more ups than downs. One downer was discovering that I had prostate cancer. Being the forever egotist, I knew I could, with the assistance of good medical personnel, beat this illness. After 40 radiation treatments, my Dr. Jacimore said she thought I was 95% cured. It has lasted several years and with prayers and God's help I will outlive cancer.

My story may seem long, but it is in short memory. Each of us with a little bit of guidance and education, can make a difference in our world, our State, our business, and our family. I have enjoyed my "try" and hope that my being on this earth has some significant meaning.

Before I finally retire (never), I will conclude my part of this story and let others write the conclusion. The ending as described in the opening paragraph.

I have included some significant facts about my existence on this earth.

Surprise 2/1/23

George Smart sent me an email stating that I was the oldest practicing Architect in North Carolina.

Born May 4, 1933, in Rocky Mount, NC

Married, Jeanette Stancil, August 21, 1954

Graduated NCSU, June 1956, Licensed Architect, January 1957

Three Children:

LeaAnn Nichols	8/29/57	UNC Charlotte
Jo Ellen (Rogers)	10/01/59	UNC Wilmington
William H II	4/15/62	NCSU

Grand Children:

Laurel (Currie)

William Rogers

Brandon Rogers

One Great Grand Child

Charlotte Grace Currie 4/9/21

Half-brother: Henry A. Thompson, Jr.

Lives in Knoxville, TN,

And has one daughter, Beth.

Services to our State, Church, Nation:

President, DKW Architects

President, NCSU Alumni Association

President, Tri-County Industries Facility

Board Trustee, Louisburg College

Trustee, EUMC

Board Trustee/ Founder, Birchwood Country Club.

Committee, Pitt Community College, Architectural department

Committee, Rocky Mount Mayor's Committee for inspection department

Committee, Rocky Mount YMCA Board

Committee, Nash Edgecombe Hall of Fame

Committee, Rocky Mount Evening Optimist

Past member Rocky Mount Elks Club

Boy Scouts of America

PHI KAPPA PHI

Airports that I have landed at during my career:

Atlanta, (Both)	Los Angeles
Augusta	Knoxville, TN
Baltimore	Ocracoke
Barbados	St. Thomas
Bermuda	Martinsburg
Billy Mitchel Buxton NC Kinston, NC	
Birmingham, Alabama	Atlantic City
Boston	Tampa
Bull Head City, Arizona	Los Angeles CA
Charleston	Elizabeth Town, Kentucky
Charleston, West Virginia	Dalton, GA
Charlotte	Santee
Chicago	Cincinnati
Cumberland, Maryland	Roxboro
Dallas, F/W	Acapulco, Mexico
Dallas, Love	Philadelphia
Denver	Richmond
Detroit	St. Martin
Greensboro	Orangeburg
Greenville, Spartanburg	Freeport
Harrisburg	Mexico City

Airports that I have landed at during my career:

Honolulu	Las Vegas
Huntington, West Virginia	
Lexington, Kentucky	
Jamaica, Kingston	Grand Cayman
Jamaica, Ochoa Rios	St. Louis
Louisville	Elizabeth City
Maui	Phoenix
Memphis	Fayetteville
Miami	Manteo
Minneapolis	
Mobile, AL	Wilmington
Moultrie, GA	Nashville, TN
Myrtle Beach, SC	Columbia, SC
Nags Head (helicopter)	
Nassau	San Juan
New Ark, Newark	Union City, TN
NY, Kennedy	Cancun
NY, La Guardia	Cozumel
Ocracoke, NC	Providence, RI
Puerto Rico	Macon Georgia
Raleigh	Pinehurst

Airports that I have landed at during my career:

San Francisco	Bluefield
South Bend	Rocky Mount 2
Sumter	Norfolk
Tarboro (helicopter)	
Washington	St. Croix
Wichita, Kansas	Paris, Charles De Gaulle
Wilson, NC	Kansas City
Winchester	
Winston-Salem	Houston, TX

Partial List of Buildings Designed by My Firms from 1957:

Boddie-Noell, Rocky Mount

Edgecombe Community College, Rocky Mount Campus, 1st Old prison Building, 4

Detention Facilities

East Carolina State University, Administrative Building, 1st Music Building, Dental Hygiene School Building, Cafeteria, Study Center, Library, Athletic Facilities, Dormitory.

Edgecombe County, Office Building, Tarboro

Englewood Shopping Center Rocky Mount

Englewood Unity Methodist Church, Rocky Mount

Halifax Community College, Theater, Technology, Science Building, Dental Hygiene School Building

Original Birchwood Clubhouse and Golf Course Design

Park Hill, Shopping Center Rocky Mount

St. Andrews Worship Building

Story Carolina Telephone, Tarboro

Western Blvd, Sprint, Tarboro

Visitors Center Manteo (Eliz.II), Ice Plant Island

Chowan College, Student Center

Bank Facilities for Planters National Bank, Centura Bank and Peoples Bank

North Carolina State University Computer Lab and Leazar Hall

North Carolina Wesleyan College, Dunn Center, Chapel, Hartness Center, Sports Complex Building, Gateway Center and Dormitories

Schools:

Edgecombe County

City of Rocky Mount

Nash Rocky Mount

Tarboro City

Weldon City

Franklin County

Hyde County, Ocracoke,

Wilson County (Hunt High School)

Halifax County

Martin County

Princeton H.S.

Roanoke Rapids City Schools

Dare County

Terrell County

Wake County

Over two hundred Telecommunication Buildings, in these states:

NC

SC

VA

KY

GA

AL

TN

W VA

Island Visited:

Aruba

Barbados

Bermuda

England

Free port

Grand Cayman

Hawaii

Jamaica

Nassau

San Juan, Puerto Rico

St. Croix

St. Martin

St. Thomas

Bucket List

+All Washington Monuments

+Atlantic Sunrise

+Cadillac's Inverted Cars, Texas

+Crossing Atlantic Ship

+Drive over San Francisco Bay Bridge

+Empire State Building Observation Deck

+Fly Concorde

+Frank Lloyd Wright Taliesin West and +Falling Water

+Grand Canyon Sunrise

+Houston Astrodome

+Kennedy Gravesite

+Key West Florida

+London St Paul Westminster

+Mississippi River Crossing

+NC Lighthouse Missing ½.

+Niagara Falls

+Notre Dame

+Nova Scotia

+Pacific Sunset

+Polio Cure

+Redwoods California

+St Louis Arch Top

+Statue of Liberty

+Yellowstone Old Faithful

-Cancer Cure

-Pyramids and the Nile

-Rome Colosseum